MW00737609

The author has not been writing for that long, but after the death of her best friend, she was inspired to share her and her friend's stories through poetry. Since January of 2020, she has been putting all her thoughts into her art and hopes to make the world a better place by doing so.

For my best friend, Mayra Roberts, and all my other friends
and family who have supported me in my endeavors.

LeAnn Lynn

WALLS

AUSTIN MACAULEY PUBLISHERS™

LONDON · CAMBRIDGE · NEW YORK · SHARJAH

Copyright © LeAnn Lynn 2023

All rights reserved. No part of this publication may be reproduced, distributed, or transmitted in any form or by any means, including photocopying, recording, or other electronic or mechanical methods, without the prior written permission of the publisher, except in the case of brief quotations embodied in critical reviews and certain other non-commercial uses permitted by copyright law. For permission requests, write to the publisher.

Any person who commits any unauthorized act in relation to this publication may be liable to criminal prosecution and civil claims for damages.

Ordering Information
Quantity sales: Special discounts are available on quantity purchases by corporations, associations, and others. For details, contact the publisher at the address below.

Publisher's Cataloging-in-Publication data
Lynn, LeAnn
Walls

ISBN 9781638292654 (Paperback)
ISBN 9781638292661 (ePub e-book)

Library of Congress Control Number: 2023903130

www.austinmacauley.com/us

First Published 2023
Austin Macauley Publishers LLC
40 Wall Street, 33rd Floor, Suite 3302
New York, NY 10005
USA

mail-usa@austinmacauley.com
+1 (646) 5125767

Acknowledgments to my friends that suffered through the first few drafts.

Table of Contents

Never Ever

Nothing in this world ever pleases you.
I try to see life from your twisted point of view,
But it never ever worked.
You're unhappy unless you're with her.
The only explanation is that you're immature.

I try so hard to get your approval.
I'm not what you wanted.
It makes me feel taunted.
I'm sorry that I disappoint you,
That is true,
But I'm not sorry for who I am.
I no longer give a damn.

I've made my decision,
Based on intuition.
You no longer control me.
It's time for me to flee.
I will escape your grasp,
I will escape your clasp.

You made me mad,
To the point that I saw red,
But now I feel free.
You made me sad,
To the point that I cried myself to sleep,
But now I feel happy.
You made me doubt myself,
To the point that I no longer believed,
But now I feel relieved.

I don't need your approval anymore.
It's time for me to finally soar.
I'm done now and forever.

Used to Be

This ain't what it used to be,
And the world can see,
That everything has changed.
My life's been rearranged—
And so, here's to what it used to be.

Your priorities are different,
I'm not as important.
Your time is spent with someone else.
I'm not as good as I was, I guess.

This ain't what it used to be,
And the world can see,
That everything has changed.
My life's been rearranged—
And so, here's to what it used to be.

I miss our talks,
And hearing all your thoughts.
What they say is true,
You don't miss them until they're someone new,
And hardly ever speak to you.
This ain't what it used to be,

And the world can see,
That everything has changed.
My life's been rearranged—
And so, here's to what it used to be.

She's like your new toy,
That caused you to destroy
Everything that we had built,
And somehow never feel the guilt.

This ain't what it used to be,
And the world can see,
That everything has changed.
My life's been rearranged—
And so, here's to what it used to be.

Scared

I'm tired of being scared to leave my house.
I don't want to feel like this anymore.
The people in charge need to do something.
It's beyond too late,
It's time to take action.

The fact that we have drills for this—
Is plain disappointing.
How about instead of making drills,
You fix the problem.
It's an easy solution,
But the people in charge don't seem to understand that.
They're all convinced that gun control won't solve the problem,
But all you have to do is look at the statistics.
Use other countries as an example.
It worked for them,
Why do you think it won't work for us?

Children shouldn't have to fight with this every day.
We are forced to walk into our own graves—
For the benefit of everyone else.
Any day now,

We could all die,

But no one blinks an eye.

If we do,

We're just going to become more names on a list.

We'll be breaking news for one day,

Then the next mass shooting will take our spot.

Stop watching the life go out of children's eyes,

Put on your big boy pants,

And do something.

I'm done waiting.

Leave Me Alone

Take the hint,
I don't want to talk to you.
Take the hint,
I don't like you.
I try and try,
But what's the point?
Because you don't seem to understand the words—
Leave me alone.

Leave me alone.
We're not friends,
And I don't want to be.
I swear,
You people never learn.
Can you not tell by my actions—
Or my words?
Do I have to spell it out for you?
Fine,
Here it is,
Leave me alone.

I wish there was a way to get away from you,
But there's nowhere else I can go.
You're everywhere.
I can't get away.
I leave,
And you come back.
LEAVE ME ALONE!

Reflection

I no longer know—
The person in the mirror.
I've never seen her before.
She's not me,
Or is she?

The girl in the reflection of my car window—
Doesn't look the same.
She's never looked out of that window before,
And she never will again,
Because tomorrow,
Someone new will be sitting in her seat.
She's not me,
Or is she?

When I look back at old pictures of myself,
I feel a longing to go back.
I looked so happy.
I had a smile on my face that would make anyone believe
the world is good.
Her life was good,
Perfect even.
She's not me,

Or is she?

I don't think that I could ever go back.
The places I used to love,
Don't feel the same anymore.
It's like a dark cloud is always hovering over me.
I want to get rid of it.
I don't like the person I've become.
I want to be happy again,
I want to feel whole again,
But I can't.
Too much has changed.
All I can do now,
Is look at my reflection,
And try to figure out who she is.

Hope

I don't want much.
I'm not a materialistic person.
I don't want a big house,
Or a fancy car.
I don't want a beach house,
Or a boat.
I just want to be happy wherever I am,
And whatever I'm doing.

I used to want the world,
But I've grown up quite a bit.
I know now,
That I don't need the world,
And I know that it's not mine to own.
The world belongs to everyone,
And the most we can do is take care of it,
And be thankful for everything that it gives us.

If I wasn't meant to be rich and famous,
I'll respect that.
If I wasn't meant to marry the love of my life and live
happily ever after,
I'll respect that.

I don't believe that you can change your fate.
You will become what you were meant to be,
And no amount of money will change that.

I hope that one day,
I'll wake up with a smile on my face,
I hope that one day,
I'll be able to accept who I am.
I hope that one day,
I'll be able to look back at my life with no regrets.
I hope that one day,
I will feel true happiness again.

Trapped

I am trapped—
In my own mind.
I can't escape.
I'm not sure how to—
Or if I should.
What if this feeling is beneficial somehow?

I'm lost in a maze.
I can't see over the hedges,
And I have no idea where the exit is.
I keep my hand on the right wall,
Because they say that's how you get out,
But it feels like I'm going in circles.

I'm a mime stuck in a box—
That my mind created.
I feel the air all around me,
As if there are walls there.
There is nothing keeping me in,
Yet I can't move.
I can't get myself out of this situation.

I am stuck—

In a trap of my own creation.

I don't remember how I got in,

Or how to get out.

The world is closing in around me.

It's getting hard to breathe,

And I feel I'm about to collapse.

Please help me get out before it's too late.

Prison

White cinderblock walls,
Red and brown bricks,
White, gray, and black tiles
Make up the physical part of this prison.
Screaming teachers,
Rude classmates,
And the stress of schoolwork
Make up the mental part of this prison.

It's painful to know that I can't escape until I graduate.
It's painful to know that I have to go here everyday
Even though I would much rather stay at home.
I try to take care of myself,
But that often gets pushed to the back of my mind.
After all,
It's been drilled into our heads that we'll be okay,
As long as we participate in school and get good grades.

I wish school didn't matter as much.
I've always wanted to spend my hours doing something that
I enjoyed doing,
But I can't.

If I don't go to school,
I won't get into a good college.
If I don't go to a good college,
I won't get a job that can support me,
And I'll end up on the streets of this unrelenting world.
Therefore, I go to school every day and I don't complain.
I can work on improving myself later.
That's not important right now.

Float Away

We seem to keep floating back to each other,
But I think it's time for me to float away—
For good.
Out with the old,
In with the new they say,
But what do they say when you want both?
What do they say when you need both?
I need you,
And I want you,
But I can't have you anymore.

Your beautiful blue eyes—
That I used to get lost in,
Are gone.
Now,
Whenever I see you,
I see red.
No more sky blue,
Just dark red.

You made me so mad.
I tried to make it work,
But you didn't seem interested.

You could've told me—
You know.
You didn't have to keep playing this game.
I would've let you go.
I would've understood.
You had to have faith in me,
But I guess you didn't.
Do you have faith now?
I let you float away.

Maybe

Does he love me? Does he not?
My stomach's in a knot.
Never understood how that would feel.
Can't use a flower for something real.
I want an answer, the real truth.
I wish I had the courage to tell you.

I want to be your good morning and goodnight.
I want to be yours and you to be mine.
All I need is a sign,
And our future could be bright.
I hold onto the idea that you like me too,
Maybe one day it will be me and you.

I love your smile,
It can make my day.
I love your laugh,
The way your cheeks wrinkle.
I love your eyes,
The way the light makes them sparkle.

I want to be your good morning and goodnight.
I want to be yours and you to be mine.
All I need is a sign,
And our future could be bright.
I hold onto the idea that you like me too,
Maybe one day it will be me and you.

I hate that I rely on you to make me happy,
And that this poem is so sappy.
I hate that I put so much faith in us.
Maybe I'll find the bravery to tell you, maybe.

I want to be your good morning and goodnight.
I want to be yours and you to be mine.
All I need is a sign,
And our future could be bright.
I hold onto the idea that you like me too.
Maybe one day it will be me and you.

Forever

I feel like I've known you forever.
I've known your name—
Since we were kids,
But we never really talked—
Until recently.

I didn't see you for a long time.
My mind managed to forget about you,
Then you came back.
It felt like you knew that I had forgotten you,
But you didn't want it to be that way.
You made yourself a part of my life,
Or I made myself a part of yours.

Now,
I can't seem to get you out of my mind.
We talk every once in a while,
When you actually show up.
I like the way you tease me.
It makes me feel loved and special.
You may not mean it the way that I think about it,
But that doesn't bother me.
You're just so mesmerizing.

I don't know if you're bad for me.

I don't know if you're going to break my heart.

I don't know if you're going to leave me scarred,

But I honestly don't care.

The idea of you is too beautiful—

For me to think logically.

So,

Will you be my forever?

My Heart Skips a Beat

My heart skips a beat when I see you.
Your shiny smile and beautiful eyes—
Make me want to be by your side until the end of days.
Do you want to be with me too?
Does your heart skip a beat when you see me?
Do you like the way my teeth shine when I smile at you?
Do you think my eyes are beautiful?
Do you?

Two years ago,
You were just a stranger,
That I never thought I would see again,
But I did see you again.
All of the sudden,
You were everywhere.
Now, we're friends, teammates,
And I care about you more than I should.
We've come so far.

Will we ever be more?
I want to,
Do you?

There's no doubt in my mind,
We could be end game.
You're the perfect daydream.
I love imagining you and me.
I think I might love you,
Do you love me too?

Confession

I have a confession to make,
I can't stop thinking about you.
You've been on my mind—
Since August of last year.
Everything you do—
Or say,
Is important to me somehow.
I overthink it all.

You don't say "good morning" or "hello,"
And I'm not sure why.
Maybe you're not awake enough yet.
Maybe you don't care enough to greet me.
Maybe you think I won't say anything back,
But I promise I will,
Every time.

You treat me like you treat everyone else.
I know you don't mean anything more than what you say,
But I still think about every word.
I think about why you said it.
I think about what made you think of it.
I think of every meaning behind it.

I know that it's unhealthy,
But I can't help it.

I want you to confess something to me.
I want you to tell me how you really feel.
I want you to tell me every thought that goes through your
head.
I want you to tell me all about your week.
I want you to tell me about the people at your school.
Most importantly,
I want you to tell me if you like me back.

Break My Heart

You took my breath away—
The first time I saw you.
You were perfect to me,
And you still are.
You don't have any flaws in my mind.

I don't really know you yet.
We just started talking,
But I have faith that you are exactly who I think you are.
You don't seem like the type of person—
That would be bad for me,
But if you are,
You have my permission to break my heart.

I'm giving you my heart.
I don't need it anymore.
You can do with it whatever you please.
You don't have to be careful.
You don't have to keep me safe.
You don't have to do anything you don't want to.
And if you decide to break my heart,
I know I'll be okay.
After all,

I'll always have the memories,
And the idea that you didn't do it on purpose.
Take my heart,
And break it.

Love, Me

I doubt that you will ever see this,
But if you do,
I have a few things to say.

First of all,
Thank you for everything that you do.
You helped me discover and accept myself—
Through your kind words and beautiful voice.
You inspired me,
And helped me believe that I can do anything.

I am so grateful that you are alive at the same time that I
am.
I don't feel the need to look like everyone else,
Because of you.
You taught me that it's okay to be different,
And instead of hiding it,
I should embrace it.
I can make a connection to every word you say,
And every song you sing.

Also,
I know this might sound weird,
But you make me feel special.
You don't even know my name,
Or know that I exist,
But I know that you care about me.
The things we share are important to me,
And I will never forget you.

Love,
Me.

An Explanation

The following seventeen poems are all about one person, my best friend. In December of 2019, my best friend committed suicide. At first, I didn't feel anything, and I had no idea how to express what was happening to me. Eventually, I got my voice back and I intend to use it for as long as I can. I met my friend when we were in seventh grade, and we stayed friends until her last moments. My goal since she died has been to raise awareness about suicide and mental illness, so more innocent lives aren't lost. This section is dedicated to my best friend. I'll always miss you.

Meeting

Met in science class
Through our mutual friends,
I loved your sass
And your confidence.
I had no idea
That you would end up meaning the world to me.

I love the day that we met—
I cherish it like I cherished you.
I'm so glad that I met you.

I'll admit I never thought I'd see you again—
That was until you showed up at camp.
Like the old ball and chain
I just couldn't keep you away.
I never thought you'd stay.

I love the day that we met—
I cherish it like I cherished you.
I'm so glad that I met you.

You were someone that I didn't have to fight for,
I knew we'd have a future,
Our friendship never felt like a chore,
I've never talked to someone like I did to you,
There wasn't anything we couldn't get through.

I love the day that we met—
I cherish it like I cherished you,
I'm so glad that I met you.

Inseparable

Our bond was unbreakable.
Nothing could tear us apart.
We could fight ten times a day,
And still smile when we see each other.
You were my favorite person to spend time with.

Science class, summer camp,
Eighth grade, lunch in high school—
We always found our way back to each other.
Time had nothing on us.
We loved each other too much to leave.

I'm so grateful for what we had,
Even if it didn't last as long as I wanted it to.
You were the best friend I've ever had.
Thank you for talking to me in seventh grade.
Without you,
I wouldn't be where I am now.
You will forever be in my heart and in my mind.
I promise not to let anyone forget you.
You and I will be inseparable.

I Thought You Were Okay

I didn't really know you,
Until we had been friends for a while.
I didn't know how much pain you were in.
You were great at hiding the sadness.
I'm so glad you finally told me the truth.

I miss when we were able to talk every day.
You were able to get everything out.
You knew I was right there,
Ready to grab your hand and walk through the flames with
you.
I made sure that you knew how much you meant to me.

You had such big dreams.
You were finally going after what you had always wanted,
And you'd be damned if anyone got in your way.
You weren't going to let their actions get to you.
You seemed happy,
Like you were determined to conquer the world.

I didn't understand at first,

Now I do.

Depression is hard to fight,

But so easy to hide.

If I only I understood before.

We could've gotten through this together.

I thought you were okay.

It's Gonna Be Alright

The sun will still come up,
The stars will still shine,
The world will still turn—
Even when I'm gone.
No one will care if I leave.
It's gonna be alright.
I'm sure that's what you thought,
But it's not true.

Sure,
The day for everyone else is still the same,
But it isn't for me anymore.
The sun comes up,
And I don't want to get out of bed,
Because I know that you won't greet me when I get to
school.
The stars shine,
And I don't want to look at them anymore,
Because I know that one of those stars—
Is you.
The world still turns,
But it doesn't feel like it,
Because my world stopped when your heart stopped.

I cared for you a lot,
And I cried so much when you left me.
I'm not alright.

I know that I'm not the only one who feels like this.
Your parents,
Your friends,
Your brothers and sisters,
Your teachers,
Your neighbors.
We all miss you, Mayra.

Rain

I'm surprised that it wasn't raining.
It felt like it should have been.
Maybe,
If it had been raining,
I wouldn't have been having such a good morning.
I wouldn't have been so happy.
I wouldn't have been distracted by the sun.
I would've been able to focus on what was wrong in the universe,
Instead of focusing on the way that the sun reflected off of the pavement.
I should've known that something was wrong.

Weather was beautiful the day after too.
It should've rained.
The rain would've washed away the tears—
That were flooding my eyes.
Maybe,
If it had been raining,
I wouldn't have felt so sad,
Because I would've known that Mother Nature was sad too.
The people around me had such a good day.
It was almost Christmas,

School had just let out for Winter Break,
Everyone was partying.
For me,
That was the second worst day of my life.
The worst day of my life—
Was the day before.

I would've felt better—
If it was raining.

Frozen in Time

The second I got the text,
I was confused.
That confusion quickly turned into concern.
My heart was racing,
I wanted to stop the tears from falling,
But I couldn't—
Because I was too scared.

I hoped that it wasn't true.
I wanted them to tell me she was wrong.
I wanted them to tell me everything was okay,
But they didn't—
Because it wasn't.
I crumbled.

I never wanted to go back in time so badly in my life.
I wanted to go back to the day before,
Or the week before.
I wanted to text you
Or call you.
I wanted you to text me
Or call me.
But you didn't—

Because you couldn't.

And in that moment,
I became frozen in time.

I'm Sorry

I can't express how sorry I am.
You needed me,
And I wasn't there for you.
No one was there for you.
I have all of these excuses,
But they don't mean anything anymore.
I realized that they were just a way—
For me to escape the guilt that I felt.
I have no valid excuse for why I wasn't there.
I'll be honest,
You weren't on my mind.
You should've been,
But you weren't,
And I'm so sorry.

I should've texted you.
I should've checked on you.
I should've been thinking about you,
But I didn't think that I had to.
You made the world believe that you were okay.
You managed to hide it all.
I like to think that you were okay,
And what you did was just an error in judgement,

But I would be naïve if I really felt that way.
You weren't okay,
And you hadn't been for a while.

I'm sorry for everything I did.
I know you didn't do that because of me,
But I am still at fault.
I knew about almost everything that was happening in your life,
And I chose to push it to the back of my mind.
I thought that my problems were more important,
But I was so wrong.
I'm sorry,
And I will be for the rest of my time on this Earth.

Drowning

I am drowning—
In a pool of my own emotions.
The water has been rising around me—
For quite a while.
I've tried to keep it all in,
But at some point the bottle was bound to explode.
Unfortunately,
The bottle broke at an inopportune time.
It shattered in front of everyone.

It felt like they were all staring at me,
But they weren't.
My vision was blurred,
But I could still see.
I looked all around for someone to hold me,
Someone to console me while I broke down,
But no one looked at me.
I assume that they were just trying to be respectful.
They knew what was going on,
Everyone did except for me.

Before I started drowning in my emotions,
I was drowning in my tears.
I'm not one to cry,
But for you,
I couldn't stop.
There are still mascara stains on my stuffed bear.
There are still tear drop stains on my notebook.
The memories from that day are all around me.
The only thing that's not around me,
Is you.

Broken

I'm broken.
I have been for months.
Ever since I lost you.
I know you didn't mean to hurt me,
But you did.
You broke me.

I can't figure out how to put myself back together.
There is no manual.
There is no tool.
I have no help.
I'm all alone in this.

No one else knows how to fix me either.
There is no guidebook.
There is no magic wand to make me feel whole again.
Everyone is trying,
But no has succeeded.
I know they mean well,
But they don't understand.
No one truly understands
Until it happens to them.
No one can feel the pain I'm in.

When Day Becomes Night

The sun goes down,
And I realize that it's nighttime.
I don't want the clock to continue ticking,
I don't want the Earth to continue spinning,
Because I know that in a few hours,
It'll be a new day.
I don't want to see tomorrow,
Because I know that you never will.

The sight of the stars in the sky is beautiful.
I love sitting on my back porch,
While I bathe in the moonlight.
At least,
I used to.
Now,
I know that you are up there with the angels,
And it hurts to look at the sky.

Once I go to sleep,
I don't want to wake up.
All of the crying that I do makes me tired,
And I wish I could sleep all day.
Every day,

I check my phone looking for a text from you.
Every day,
I check Instagram hoping that you posted something while
I was asleep,
But you never do.
You haven't texted me in three months.
You haven't posted anything on social media in three
months.

I don't know why I keep doing this to myself.
I guess the idea of you still being here keeps me going.
I need to find something else to inspire me,
But I don't want to.
I don't want to forget you—
When night becomes day,
Or day becomes night.

The Tears I've Cried

The tears I've cried—
Are all for you.

When I wake up,
When I see the bracelet you gave me,
When I see pictures of you,
When I see your Instagram,
When I read over our texts,
When I listen to that song,
When I see your crush,
When I think about you,
When I write about you,
I can't seem to stop the tears from falling.

My face turns red,
And my vision gets blurry.
My nose starts to run,
And my lips begin to quiver.
I get goosebumps on my arms,
And my whole body shakes.
All of this happens before I finally break down.

The tears I've cried,
And continue to cry,
Are all for you.

Lost

I don't know where I am,
I haven't for a while.
It's like,
The second I got the news,
I was transported to some foreign island.
There are no maps or guides,
There's just darkness.

At first,
I was scared,
But now I'm used to it.
I wasn't always able to be by myself,
But now it doesn't bother me.
In fact,
I prefer to be alone.
When I'm alone,
I can cry.
I can search my mind for the right words to express how I
feel.
I can scroll through our old texts without someone asking
me what I'm doing.

When I'm with other people,
I can't do those things,
I'm too busy making sure that the people around me are
okay.

I'm lost,
And I can't find my way out.
I've been going in circles for as long as I can remember.
I recognize the things around me,
But they don't mean anything.
They can't tell me how to get out of here,
So,
I will stay lost—
Until someone finds me.

Out of Reach

You're out of my reach.
I try to hug you.
I try to sit with you.
I try to talk to you.
I just want to be near you,
But you're too far away.

You're out of my reach.
I miss your smile.
I miss your laugh.
I miss your sarcasm.
I want it all back,
But you're gone.

You're out of my reach.
I hope you're okay.
I hope you're no longer in pain.
I hope you're happy.
I still love you,
Even if you're not with me.

You're out of my reach.
I wish I could've been enough to keep you here.
I wish you told me how you truly felt.
I wish I could've hugged you one more time.
But most of all,
I wish you the best wherever you are.

Everyday

My whole life is different.
I don't like doing the things that I used to do all the time.
I don't like singing,
I don't dream of becoming a pop star.
I don't like doing my hair—
Or my makeup anymore.
All of the things that I enjoyed—
When you were alive,
Are tarnished with the knowledge that you aren't here
anymore.

People tell me it's normal.
Everything that I'm feeling is OKAY to feel.
Guilt, remorse,
Anger, sadness;
Everyone feels like that after something so traumatic
happens,
But I've never been like everyone else.
I shouldn't feel guilt,
I know that I wasn't the reason you were depressed.
I shouldn't feel remorse,
There is no way I could've known that you were going to
do that.

I shouldn't feel anger,

How you felt wasn't your fault.

I shouldn't feel sadness,

I know that you're no longer in pain,

I know that you're happy now wherever you are.

But, as much as I don't like it,

I let myself feel those things,

Because in the end, it makes me feel better.

Those are the thoughts that go through my mind every day.

Every day,

I think of you,

I think about how it used to be,

I think about what our future would've been like,

I think of the people you left behind,

I think about what my life will be like now that you're gone.

Every day,

You are on my mind.

What Do I Do Now?

You left me too soon.
You were supposed to be with me—
Until we got old and wrinkly.
We were supposed to spend our whole lives together.
Sure, we weren't going to live forever,
But you had so much of your life ahead of you.
Seventeen was too soon.

I feel like I can't do anything—
Now that you're gone.
For days,
I didn't know how to smile.
For weeks,
I couldn't express how I felt.
I used to be able to do those things easily,
But now I can't.

What do I do now that I can't talk to you?
What do I do now that we can't have any more sleepovers?
What do I do now that we can't get ready for any more dances together?
What do I do now that I can't tell you about my weekend?

What do I do now that I can't hear you fantasize over your future?

What do I do now that we can't live together when we graduate?

What do I do now that I can't see your face light up when you laugh?

What do I do now that I can't roll my eyes at the stupid jokes you make?

What do I do now that you're not by my side?

What do I do now?

Closure

I need something to soothe my mind.
I need something to calm myself down.
I need something to convince me that you're gone,
Despite my wish that you are still here.

I haven't seen your room,
Or even your house for two months.
We didn't hang out at your house very much,
But I have the urge to go visit you.
It's like my heart is trying to convince my brain that it's not true.
My brain knows what really happened and why it did,
But my heart refuses to admit it.
I'm in denial.

Even though I don't want to accept that you're gone,
I know that I need to.
I need to go to your funeral.
I need to go to your memorial service.
I need to see a huge picture of you in the front of a funeral home.
I need to see a room filled with flowers that people sent to you.

It may sound morbid,

But the battle between my heart and my head—

Is eating me alive.

I need to know for sure that you're not going to text me,

And tell me it was all a joke,

And that you're okay.

I know those thoughts seem irrational,

But I can't help the way I feel.

I need closure.

Goodbye

Goodbye to—
My best friend,
My maid of honor,
My oldest friend,
My children's aunt.

Goodbye to—
A daughter,
A sister,
A friend,
A future celebrity.

Goodbye to—
The best mean person,
The girl who never failed to make me laugh,
The friend I saw a future with,
The person I could always count on.

I know you meant a lot to a lot of people,
Because I was one of those people.
I would do anything to bring you back,
But that's not how this works.
You didn't want to be here anymore,

And I wouldn't be your friend if I wished for you to suffer any longer,
So, I have one last thing to say...
Goodbye.

Here's a Few More...

The remainder of the poems were written a while ago. I wrote these when I dreamed of becoming a singer, so they were intended to be songs. I don't have the same dreams, so I decided to add them to this poetry collection. The feelings that these poems revolve around are long gone, and I've liked being able to look back at my past. I've grown and changed a lot since these were written. Some changes were good, other changes were bad, but they've all led me to where I am now. All of these emotions made me who I am, and I'm proud of who I've become. These poems hold a special part in my heart, because of everything I've been through. Creating these made me realize my love for writing and my dream of becoming an author. I hope that the future generation has the same opportunities that I did, and I hope that they are able to discover who they really are through whatever creative outlet they find the most helpful and enjoyable. With that being said, please enjoy the remainder of the poems in this collection.

I Quit

I always do what makes me happy,
But you act snappy.
You cause me to doubt myself.
That was a red flag in itself.
It may be weird, but who cares.

I'm tired of being your punching bag.
I'm tired of telling you I'm okay.
I'm not okay.
I'm angry, I'm sad, and it's your fault.
I'm tired of taking your assault.
I'm done, I quit.

I'm always there for you.
My name is always in view.
Sometimes I need you, but you're nowhere to be found.
You never seem to be around.
Our relationship isn't healthy.

You take it all out on me.

It's time to set myself free.

I'm still here, but I won't be for much longer.

I'm finally stronger.

Take me in while you can,

'Cause I'm leaving.

Blinded

I trusted you.
I thought what you said was true.
If only I knew,
That you would stab me in the back.
I tried to backtrack,
But I still can't figure out what made you want to attack.

The smile on my face was fake;
Just like your attitude.
All you did was take.
You changed how other people were viewed,
And it was all for your own benefit.
You had to be number one,
And you didn't care who you stepped on.

You seemed to have good intentions.
You caused so much tension.
You just wanted attention.
I was so wrong.
You made me feel like I belong,
You fooled me for so long.

What makes you think that anything you did was okay?
I was your prey.
I was hurt if I ever got in your way.
I learned the lesson early on,
That your heart was black.
Thank God you're gone.

You stepped on me,
And who knows how many others.
Now I'm carefree,
Cause I got far away from you.

Rearview Mirror

You're in my past—
I don't care what you do, I don't care what you say.
I couldn't care less about you.

I still remember everything but chose to block it out.
It was hard to erase you.
You had a huge impact on my life—
But I did, I got rid of you.

We had sleepovers,
We played games at school,
You encouraged me to do what makes me happy,
So I did, and now all I have to say is goodbye.

You suddenly didn't want to sit with me.
You refused to talk to me or work with me.
I don't know what I did,
Or what happened during the summer we were apart,
But I do know you changed, and it wasn't for the better.

You're in my past.

I don't care what you do,

I don't care what you say.

The day you crossed me is the day I forgot you.

All you are is a picture in the rearview mirror,

A picture in my rearview mirror.

Don't Deserve Me

You made me feel wanted.
You told me I was what you were looking for.
That sound leaves me haunted.
You caused a war,
Within my own mind.
You were so quick to compliment.
Your words made me blind.
You made me believe you.

You don't deserve to know I feel.
You don't deserve my tears.
What we had wasn't real.
You don't deserve the attention.
You don't deserve my memories.
You don't deserve this confession.
I deserve to move past you.
I deserve to get this off my chest.
You never deserved me.

How could you think it's okay to treat me like that?
You broke me apart.
You played me and I lost my trust in you.
I'm not another toy for your toy box.
I'm not another object for you to brag about.
I'm not another loop on your belt.
I'm not another name on a list.

Close My Eyes

When I close my eyes, I see the past.
All the memories start flooding back.
Everything that I loved completely wiped away,
But they still live in my mind.
When I close my eyes, it all comes back.

Running down the stairs on Christmas morning.
I wish I got more of a warning,
That it would be taken from me.
I used to climb on the small tree,
Right in the center of everything.
I wouldn't trade that for the world.

I remember playing in the leaves with the dog,
And trying to start a fashion blog.
Sledding down the hills in recycling bins.
We sure did some strange things.
Hanging with the kids down the road.
Had the time of my life but I lost it.

Had the fence put up by my uncle,
Can't tell you how many times I hurt my ankle.
All the memories good and bad,
Could never truly make me mad.

Watched our movies in the living room.
My mother loved watching the roses bloom.
She put a rose in my hair before I performed;
That's when my love for music formed.

When I close my eyes, I see the past.
All the memories start flooding back.
Everything that I loved completely wiped away,
But they still live in my mind.
When I close my eyes, it all comes back.
When I close my eyes—

CPSIA information can be obtained
at www.ICGtesting.com
Printed in the USA
LVHW022049140423
744403LV00010B/501

9 781638 292654